Processing Systems Change in Banking
(causes and effects)

Mercy Mwila Kunda
and
Julius B Goode

ISBN:10:1512276464
ISBN-13:978 1512276466

DEDICATION

To all non-bankers, who just want to have a slight idea of what happens in banks, and why.

CONTENTS

ACKNOWLEDGEMENTS

1. Amedeo (2012): Centralization and Accountability Theory and Evidence

2. Adrian Perez (2013): Centralized Treasury Yields Benefits

3. Allan C Carison (2010): Centralization and Principles

4. Andy Ponsford, JP Morgan and Seamus De Souza (2006): Centralization and Rationalization

5. Asheley D Manker (2003): Centralization Fayol's Principle Lesson and Quiz

6. Asma Zaineb (2011): Centralization in an organization, advantages and disadvantages

7. Dimensional data (2011): Centralization and standardization of Network Operations

8. Donald Kisilu Kombo and Dellno L. A. Tromp (2009): Proposal and Thesis Writing 7th Edition

9. Dr Petr Polak and Ivan Klusace K (2010): Centralization of Treasury Management 1st edition

10. Edward Sweeney (2001): The Impact of Centralized Distribution on Distributors and Agents

11. Edward Taylor Mysis Global Processing IT (2013) Banks now able to centralize their Trade Finance Operations

12. Eric Maskin (1999): From centralization to the market theory

13. Financial Insights case study (2008): Centralization systems support

14. Godfrey Yeung (2012): Centralization and Marginalization; The Chinese banking industry in reform

15. Janusz G Ziielinski Economics of Planning (1963): Centralization and Decentralization in Decision Making

16. Jim Riley (2012): Managing People, Centralization organization structures

17. John Herrick and Michael Gallanis Treasury strategies (2010): The Pros and Cons of Centralization

18. KPMG cutting through complexity (2012): Optimizing banking operating models.

19. Lesley white and Bruce Meuli, Bank of America Merrill Lynch (2013): The Evolution of shared service centres

20. Mangwengwende, Tadiwanashe Mukudzeyi (2010): The relationship between bank concentration and Interest rates

21. Mark Saunders (2009): Research methods for business students 5th Edition

22. Niki Glaveli and Stella Kufidu (2011): A Comparative analysis of the impact of environmental change

23. Omo Aregbeyen and Jumoke Olufemi (2011): The impact of recapitalization and consolidation of banks

24. Patrick Jonson, Martin Romberg and Stephen Holmberg (2013): Centralized supply chain planning, An International Journal Vol. 18

25. Peter Klibanoff and Michael Poitevin (2013): A theory of (de) centralization

26. Prof. Dr. Joachim Moller and Prof. Dr. Lutz Arnold (2004): Employment and welfare effects of centralization

27. Robert Hunt (2000): SBI World's largest centralized core processing implementation

28. Steven A Rhoades (1997): The efficiency effects of bank mergers

29. Summit Energy services (2010): Clearing the hurdles to energy management centralization

30. Thorsten Beck, Asli Demirgue Kunt and Ross Kenne (2003): Bank concentration

31. Tremenos case study (2006): Schcroder Private Banking, three perspective on IT centralization

32. Vijay Alexander and Eupen Thomas (2008): Combining process and technology to achieve agility.

Books by Julius B Goode

The Rhodesian Project

A Place in the Sun

The Kaiser Wilhelm Strasse Protocol

…if you ever miss me…

Some day in the summertime

One for you, two for me.

A spy like you

Dirty fingers in the pie

1-BRIEF HISTORICAL BACKGROUND

Changes in the banking sector have always been a constant feature. In fact, it can be said to be just about the only one. The changes have been in most part been necessitated by the environment in which banks operate.

If we may take an example of Zambia, during the period from the late 1970s up to the 1990s, the economy of the country was in dire straits and very volatile. Drastic movements in economic indicators had a very adverse effect on the banking sector. An example would be the foreign exchange rate, of the Kwacha against the United States dollar. Changes in the rate over the period were as follows;

1978	0.8
1983	1.26
1985	7.79
1990	30.29

1993   482.76

1996   1203.71

The significance of this cannot be overemphasized. One must remember that all the major banks in the country, except for Zambia National Commercial Bank, were foreign owned. Their profitability was seen in terms of either the United States dollar or the British pound. During the period highlighted above, profits remitted to the parent banks overseas suffered a major decline. Any erosion in the value of the local currency was translated into erosion of profit figures when the conversion was done to the foreign currency.

One must understand that the country was going through a lot of economic difficulties. Export earnings were on the decline and there was a shortage of dollar and pound on the market. Figures stated above were far lower than the ones prevailing in the booming black market in which a lot of foreign cash transactions took place and the available currencies obtained. In most cases, the black market rates were double the official ones. This black market trade occurring outside the banking sector had the effect of syphoning money out of the sector. Since revenues from such trade were kept in homes, cash deposits and balances on bank accounts saw a significant reduction.

Efforts to control the black market had proved futile over the years, though a sudden currency note change during one of the economic reforms in the 1980s, announced to last for a duration of only a week, made those involved in the trade lose fortunes. They were left with trunks and suitcases of useless Kwacha notes that they failed to change in banks. The government had set a limit on the amount of cash that a person could change over the counter, a very small drop in the ocean as compared to amounts accumulated over the years.

A reduction in cash deposits and lowering of bank balances which were attributed mainly to the black market trade meant that there was less money for banks to lend out. Since most of the banks' income comes from interest and commissions earned on loans to customers, the banks' profitability was therefore affected.

The other factor that had an effect on the banks' profitability during the period was the high rate of inflation. Inflation is defined as a persistent rise in the general level of prices related to an increase in the volume of money and resulting in the loss of value of the currency. This probably has a greater impact on banks which has large personal customer portfolios.

Inflation affects household. The more money a household spends on food and other commodities, the less there is to save and deposit in the accounts. The rate of inflation in 1980 was around 11%. In 1985 it rose to 37%, 1990 to 110%. It peaked in 1993 at nearly 190%. Needless to say, this had a severe effect on banks' retail customer account portfolio.

During this period, inflation was in a large part triggered by a severe shortage of essential commodities. What was smuggled into the country could only be bought on the black market at exorbitant prices. This seriously affected customers' ability to save money.

To expand the environmental picture just a little bit more, it is important to look at the performance of the copper mines in the country.

Copper production over the period of time declined significantly. Copper was and remains the mainstay of Zambia's economy. Any drop in production or leakage in income has a multiplier effect. A lot of companies and industries feed off the mines. When a change occurs in the mining sector, adverse or otherwise, it is felt immediately, especially on the Copperbelt Province.

The significance of the decline can be highlighted by examining the quantities of copper exports (in a thousand metric tonnes) over the period;

1983   864

1985   674

1990   459

1993   436

1996   303

Declining copper mineral exports meant declining foreign

currency revenues. What needs to be examined further is the reason for the deteriorating foreign exchange rate when, on the world market, the price of the commodity over the period was quite high. Clearly, there was a significant income leakage somewhere.

The drop in profitability in the mines seemed a good enough reason for shareholders to call for a review of operations, resulting in staff number rationalization and closing down of unprofitable mine shafts altogether. This had a domino effect on other industries, the banking sector included. In towns where mine shafts were closed, banks followed suit and closed branches, or at the very least, cut costs by reducing operations, cutting the number of operating hours of the branch, and/or reduced staff numbers. The country's rural areas probably suffered the most, with almost all the banks pulling out, to concentrate along the line of rail. Only Zambia National Commercial Bank, among the major banks, maintained a continuous presence in the rural areas, though this was most likely because the government has a hand in the shareholding and could therefore influence bank policy.

These branch closures had a dire effect on bank/customer relationships. Some customers had to travel from one town to another, at great cost, to access funds on their accounts. They often found that by the time they had managed to get to the branch, it was past closing time. Exodus of customers from these banks soon followed, and relationships were never restored even after the branches had been re-opened in these towns when the country's economy improved.

What should also not be forgotten is that miners who were laid off and companies which no longer had contracts with the mines had in most cases gotten loans and advances from banks. This period witnessed banks having a high volume of non-performing loans in their books. Recovery of these loans proved costly. Dedicated departments were set up, to follow up the customers. These follow ups were not just by telephone, but with personal visits as well. This meant incurring further costs, relating to both transport and personal expenses.

The country had by then exchange control regulations in place, to monitor foreign currency inflows and outflows. The foreign exchange rate was fixed by government, acting through the central bank.

The fixed foreign exchange rate pegged the value of the Kwacha to the United States dollar. This works out well as long as the economy is in a good state and the country's balance of payment (relating to revenues of exports against expenditure on import) is in credit. However, as was the case in Zambia, when the value and amount of exports falls, the **balance of payment goes into deficit.**

The resultant situation was that the fall in revenue from exports brought about a shortage of foreign currency. Demand became far more than the supply. The official exchange rate became grossly overvalued, and a more realistic exchange rate appeared on the ever growing black market. This attracted foreign currency away from the official market, with dire consequences to the economy.

A fixed foreign exchange rate may, however, be beneficial in long term strategic planning. When the country was on a fixed foreign exchange rate, with exchange control regulations in place, it can be argued that bank management was able to put in place long term plans, and then monitor the income from loans and other advances.

It is worth noting that for bankers, marketing of banking products was never thought of then. The brand names of banks sold themselves. It was the customer who came to the banks seeking to be served, not the other way round. Marketing of bank products therefore was not a priority, though this was to change later.

During this same period, a policy was introduced to hold weekly auctioning of foreign currency at Bank of Zambia. This was meant to provide transparency in the way that allocation of foreign currency to the public was done.

The Foreign Exchange Management Committee (FEMAC) was set up to receive and analyze bids for foreign exchange. These bids had to come through the banks, with all the relevant import documentation attached to support them.

The auctioning ran for an approximate period of two years, ending in early 1987.

One option open to government during periods when a shortage of foreign currency is being experienced is to use reserves of foreign currency or borrowing foreign currency from overseas. Borrowing from overseas brings about foreign debt, which in the long run can prove to be detrimental to the economy, as it did with Zambia.

The other option would be putting in place an enforced reduction in demand for imports, by banning importation of certain goods and services. The government can also ration the amount of foreign exchange made available to the public, except maybe to the industries and business houses considered essential to the effective running of the country's economy.

Coming to the banking sector, one must also bear in mind that during the period in question, there were only four major banks. The picture changed dramatically with the liberalization of both the economy and the banking sector. More players came into the market. By 1995, there were more than twenty banks in the country from the previous four, with more planning to come in.

Competition between the financial institutions became very stiff, with all going into the market to gain as much foothold as possible. Innovation as regards financial instruments came into play. In some cases, procedures were greatly eased, especially for opening accounts. This led to the accounts being opened faster by new banks, and as a way of attracting customers, soft loans given out without taking the necessary precautions. This move was to backfire later on, when the economy worsened and banks faced liquidity challenges precipitated by non-performing loans. The resultant effect was that some banks failed to meet regulatory requirements set by the central bank. By 2001, the nine commercial banks listed below had failed.

1-African Commercial Bank Limited
2-Bank of Credit and Commerce International
3-Commerce Bank Limited
4-Credit Africa Bank Limited
5-First Merchant Bank Zambia Limited
6-Manifold Investment Bank Limited
7-Meridien BIAO Bank
8-Prudence Bank Limited
9-Union Bank Zambia Limited

The loss of confidence and trust in local banks was immeasurable. It took time for customers to go back to opening accounts with them, because of the fear that sooner or later, all the local banks would collapse, dragging people's life savings down with them. What eventually helped to take customers back to the local banks in the long run were the low balances required to open and maintain accounts, as compared to foreign owned banks, as well as low maintenance fees that these banks were charging for their accounts.

With the liberalization of the economy came a floating foreign exchange rate policy. The value of the foreign currency was then determined by the market forces of supply and demand. A look at the exchange rates for the period from 1990 to 1996 shows just how severe the resultant effect was. As it may be expected, profitability of foreign owned banks dropped drastically, since it is denominated in foreign currency when remittances are made out of the country to their controlling head offices.

Pressure thus mounted on bank management to ensure that levels of profitability were not only maintained, but increased. Bank officials often complained of seemingly impossible performance targets given to them, the complaints stretching from top management right down to the clerk on the Enquiries counters. Some banks even introduced incentives such as bonuses, to coax high performance from staff.

Banks were forced to look at various options of maintaining profitability. Marketing strategies were put in place and cost cutting measures introduced. There was a general overhaul of banking operations, with more staff being deployed in the front office to deal with customer service and marketing demands, while back office operations, which did not generate any income, shrunk in staff numbers. In the banks' head offices, new marketing departments sprung up, headed by specialists other than traditional bankers. Top advertisers and marketers soon found themselves moving from their traditional industries to try out their skills in the banking sector.

Cost cutting strategies in Zambian banks have focused mainly on achieving optimum efficiency through automation of most processes and centralizing the processing of transactions. Banks have invested heavily in technology. The availability of packaged software has made multi-tasking possible, and there is bound to be less and less reliance on human intervention in most transaction processing. It may be of interest to note that software development costs can be capitalized and treated as fixed assets, especially if the software is for internal use, that is, acquired or developed only for the internal needs of the business. Examples of such needs are;

-accounting systems

-cash management tracking systems

-membership tracking systems

-production automation systems.

Acquisition of such software therefore adds value to the company.

It is now possible to move documents electronically, by e-mail and image capturing. This has cut down immense costs relating to use of paper. It is worth noting that even record keeping has gone digital, facilitating reduction in the size of storage space. Records that used to fill up warehouses in box folders and files are now being stored on DVDs.

One process that has seen near automation is cash dispensing. It was traditional to see banking halls overcrowded during month ends, when companies pay salaries and wages to their workers. However, bank accounts in some towns are just used as pay points, with salaries being withdrawn in their entirety, leaving only the minimum balance.

Banks need funds which are kept on accounts for long periods of time, funds which can then be lent out to earn interest and commissions. If only the minimum balances are kept on the accounts, maintenance of these accounts end up being costly, taking into account the cost of processing of salaries schedules and expenses incurred during the month ends when staff members have to work even during lunch hour.

Cost reduction was achieved through introduction of automated teller machines (ATMs). Long queues have been transferred from banking halls as a result. Outsourcing of ATM maintenance has further freed bank staff to concentrate on sales and customer service. Advances in ATM operating software will enable cash deposits to be made as well, further reducing the need for customers to go to the bank.

Banks have also been able to achieve economies of scale by partnering with international companies in the issuance of credit and debit cards. It has worked to the customers' advantage. It is very convenient to be able to withdraw funds from any ATM machine, irrespective of which bank installed it.

Many banks are realizing that they need to react more quickly to business and market changes by centralizing their processes or merging their main departments.

Process centralization, which conveys the idea of consolidation of processes, amalgamating, aggregating and integration, has also been viewed as mapping multiple processes and data of an organization and generating a comprehensive integrative structure is on the increase in the recent decades (Klaus et al., 2000).

Banks may also centralize their processes for various reasons may include the need to comply with the rapidly evolving regulatory demands, imposed perhaps by the central bank. Others, as stated before, see centralization of processes as a way to reduce their cost base and improve their competitiveness.

One aspect which has often been overlooked is the effect that process centralization and/or departmental mergers in the banking industry has on employees, customers and the organization itself. There is therefore need to identify driving factors for centralization and/or departmental mergers and carrying out of an analysis on the effect they have on employees and customers, highlight challenges and benefits that may come with centralization of processes, and ultimately determine the best way to carry out a process centralization that should benefit all parties involved.

Ever since the financial crisis of 2008, authorities around the world have been determined to avoid a repeat of the scenario, resulting in a lot of regulatory changes being implemented. The aim has been to tighten up regulation and avoiding another 'too big to fail' situation where governments are forced to use public funds to prop up failing financial institutions.

These global regulations and competitive pressures in the banking industry are making it increasingly important to have a core banking system that can respond to changes in the ever dynamic market, allowing banks to offer clients highly targeted products that have a fast time to market. It is also becoming more important to have a centralized system that can take advantage of synergies and provide a speedy view of banks' operations (Parveen, 2008).

The guiding philosophy that has been used in justifying centralization is, according to a KPMG paper in 2012, 'Economies of scale through centralization of services on a national, regional or global level, added to exploitation of internal synergies through consolidation of core systems and horizontally integrated operations centres, guarantees increased efficiency'

Centralization of processes is thus happening globally in the banking industry. In Zambia, centralization of processes has and is taking place in many commercial banks. The payment system is one example.

In an effort to reform and enhance the efficiency of the payments system, the Bank of Zambia initiated a study of payment systems within the region in 1993, and by 1995 was working together with the Bankers' Association of Zambia on reforming the Zambian payment systems. In 1999 the

Electronic Clearing House was established in Zambia as an independent entity operating at two clearing centres. In the southern region, clearing was done at the Lusaka Electronic Clearing House and in the northern region at the Kitwe Electronic Clearing House.

The objective of the reform was to formalize an efficient payments, clearing and settlement system for the Zambian financial system within a clear legal framework. The following were some of the measures that were implemented to make the National Payments System more efficient and reliable;

1- The establishment of electronic clearing of cheques. Zambia Clearing House rules were redrafted, and improvement made regarding security of cheque paper. There was also the introduction of machine readable cheques, a reduction in the number of days taken to clear cheques, as well as improvements in the banks' internal processing procedures.

2- As an additional measure to enhance improvements, operations at Kitwe Electronic Clearing Centre were later moved to the Lusaka Electronic Clearing House. This was after the cheque truncation system was introduced. This left the Kitwe Electronic Clearing Centre as a disaster recovery centre only.

Despite a growing number of banks opting for process centralization and merging of their main departments, little has been done to analyze the effect of process centralization on the other parties involved, which are the customers and employees. The main driving force behind centralization of processes appears to be shareholder concerns. Employee and customer concerns appear secondary. It must be highlighted that for any project to achieve a good measure of success, concerns of all parties must be addressed and benefits resulting from the project communicated to all concerned parties.

A lot of anxiety often accompanies any hint of process change that might lead to job losses. It may be worth noting that most of the bankers have no skills outside banking. Until the late 1990s, banks had a policy of not allowing workers to engage in any form of business, so as to avoid conflict of interest issues. The fear of the affected workers is therefore understandable.

When job losses occur, such as retrenchments or early retirements, some banks make efforts to help the workers make the transition to life outside banking by organizing seminars during which people who had gone through the same experience offer their advice and give tips as how to start small businesses. Tips on entrepreneurship often prove to be very useful during these meetings.

2-THE NATIONAL PAYMENT SYSTEM

A more comprehensive look at the National Payment System is probably necessary.

Ever since the central bank put in place a strategy to reform the national payment system, a lot of improvements have been made. The reformation of the system began in earnest in 1995, when it became apparent that with the liberalization of the economy, a better payment system had to be put in place. Flaws were discovered in the system that not only caused delays in payments being effected, but also contributed to financial institutions being exposed to risky positions.

The main instruments of payments were cheques, bank drafts, manager's cheques, and bankers' payments. There were also mail and telegraphic transfers, as well as standing orders. Business men had the letter of credit facility for international trade.

Processing of these instruments was manual, a process that was found to be slow. There was a lot of pressure on the payment system, brought about by the demands of the liberalized economy.

The mostly widely used payment instrument was the cheque, but it had deficiencies that made it quite risky. Not only was it susceptible to fraudulent use, because of not having strong enough security features, but it was also abused by unscrupulous businessmen who took advantage of delays in the clearing system. This abuse invariably left banks exposed to risks of financial loss.

Before the financial institutions upgraded their computer systems, cheques had to be cleared by branches on which they were drawn. If, for instances, a businessman based in Lusaka and having an account with Bank A with a branch in Lusaka, received a cheque drawn on a branch of Bank B, located in Livingstone, he had to wait for it to be physically taken to the branch in Livingstone before he could receive cleared funds. This process could take up to four days. Clearing periods varied according to the location of the branches on which the cheques are drawn. Branches along the line of rail had shorter periods, while those away from the cities could have clearing periods of up to a week.

The long clearing period of cheques could be taken advantage. A businessman, after opening accounts in different towns or different banks, could deposit a cheque drawn on an account which he knew had insufficient funds. He would then negotiate with the bank manager to draw funds against the uncleared cheque. The term 'kite flying' describes this tactic. It is actually a form of cheque fraud, taking advantage of non-existent funds in another account. This is a way of obtaining unauthorized credit.

Dishonouring of cheques soon became so rampant during the early days of the liberalized economy that use of the instrument decreased significantly. Businesses could only accept them from people that they trusted, and sometimes only after getting confirmation from banks where the cheques were drawn.

Confirmation of these cheques was not really official, because of the oath of secrecy that bank officials sign. It usually took place between bank officials who knew each other. They were aware of the fact that when confirming a cheque, they were treading on very thin ice. Their actions might be seen as disclosing confidential information on a customer's account. The usual practice was to request if the amount of the cheque could be met by the balance on the account if it was presented at that time, without asking what the balance was on the account. The response was usually conditional, given on the assumption that all other technicalities on the cheque were correct, and assuming that no other cheques were presented to deplete the balance on the account.

Some customers submitted confirmation lists to banks, stating the amounts and payees of all the cheques that had been issued for a period. This was a simple safeguard against fraud. Bank officials were then in a position to get in touch with the customer in a case where there was an anomaly, or simply dishonoured the cheque if it was not on the list.

There were certain business transactions where personal cheques could not be accepted. In such a case, a manager's cheque was asked for. This is a cheque drawn on a bank's own account, issued and signed by branch management. The process of obtaining a manager's cheque is that a customer presents a cheque drawn on a personal account to the bank. The bank then debits the personal account and credits its own internal account. It then issues a cheque of its own, drawn on the internal account.

Manager's cheques were, and are as good as cash, since they are drawn on the bank's own account.

Cheque abuse and kite flying were only curbed or at least brought under control when the payment system was reformed, with banks upgrading their computer system to ensure that cheque clearing and funds transfers were effected immediately. This brings to mind one advantage of centralization of processes. By having one cheque processing centre and an easily accessible and well maintained data base, a cheque can be drawn on any branch of a bank within the country and still be cleared, since all the customers' information is readily available.

Reformation of the clearing system brought in new requirements as regarding the quality and format of cheques. The decision to have an advanced electronic payment system meant adding other features on the cheques. In addition to existing security markings, which are only visible under ultra violet light, it was made mandatory to have printers of cheque books include the magnetic ink character recognition code, the MICR line. This is printed at the bottom of the cheque. Banks that did not comply with this by advising their customers to order the new cheque leaves were charged a penalty fee. Any cheque that did not have the new features and was picked up during the interbank clearing process was dishonoured. This speeded up the process of reforming the payment system, as obsolete cheques were soon taken out of circulation.

This technology made it easy to process and clear cheques. In fact, the technology was applied to deposit slips as well. The MICR line includes details such as the bank code, bank account number, cheque number, and a control indicator. The cheque amount is also encoded by the person processing the voucher. These details also facilitate sorting of vouchers during processing.

To make the sorting of vouchers possible, the clearing house produced a list of codes by which individual banks could be identified. These sort codes are unique in that there is a code for each bank, each branch and the town or city in which they are located. There are other codes which identify a voucher, whether it is a personal cheque, or a company cheque. Managers' cheques also have their own unique digit.

On deposit slips, there are codes distinguishing cash deposits from cheque deposits.

To be able to read details of these vouchers, MICR readers were brought into the system to scan and transmit the information directly into the banks' database for storage and processing.

MICR readers work much the same way as old tape recorders did. There is a read head that recognizes magnetic characters of the cheques, and these are transformed into electronic form that is then identified by the system. One advantage of the magnetic characters on the cheque is that they can be read even if they are obscured by the customer's signature, or by a bank stamp. Banks have however been advised not to accept any cheque that has any mark in the MICR line, just to avoid any errors when the cheque is passed through the reader.

The main aim of having all these changes made to the cheque was to facilitate introduction of cheque truncation. Under this system, details of the cheque are captured by the MICR reader, including the electronic image. These are then transmitted in an electronic file to the bank on which the cheque is drawn. In addition to details of the cheque, the presenting bank details are also transmitted. There is no physical movement of the cheque itself.

Paying of the cheque is done using the image. The bank ensures that technicalities on the cheque are correct, the main features being the signature, the amount in words and figure, and the date. Any anomaly in these details will result in the cheque being dishonoured. The cheque will also be unpaid if there are insufficient funds on the account, since the system is automated.

With the introduction of cheque truncation came the Automated Clearing House, operated by the central bank. This is a computer based clearing and settlement facility, where all the transactions, both debits and credits, are netted off to show each participating bank's current account position. Each financial institution's account is held by the central bank.

In the past, settlement of bank positions was cumbersome and prone to errors. The country was divided in regions, and each region had a clearing house where representatives of banks met to physically exchange cheques and credit vouchers. The amounts were netted off, and each representative then went back to their respective banks to advise their head office treasury departments. As it can be noted, mistakes were made, and the central bank was often advised of wrong bank balances. Computerization of the system eliminated all these errors.

Transformation of the payment system also introduced the process of DDACC. (Direct Debit and Credit Clearing). This is an electronic funds transfer which bank customers can use to credit or debit their clients' accounts directly. It is an efficient way to collect regularly occurring payments. Local authorities, public utilities and insurance companies can use this facility to collect payments from their customers. It is also a very efficient facility for making salary payments. As long as details are correct, the accounts are credited or debited the same day, once banks run the electronic files.

Introduction of DDACC has rendered some of the payment instruments obsolete, mail transfers and banker's payments being good examples. These were once used to transfer funds between branches of a bank, and between banks. They were delivered by post or taken by hand to the beneficiary banks or branches.

The other instrument which was also susceptible to fraud was the telegraphic transfer. These were instructions sent between banks, to credit customer accounts. The messages were often intercepted whilst in transit, and beneficiary details changed. Only effective coding of the messages stopped this fraudulent activity. Transfers, especially international one, are now done through SWIFT (Society for Worldwide Interbank Financial Telecommunication). This is an international cooperative through which financial institutions send secure messages.

The organization has standardized forms which banks and other financial institutions use to code their messages and fund transfer requests. All financial institutions and their respective branches have SWIFT codes, ensuring that once the remitter inputs the codes and transmits the electronic file, funds are going to be received. It has proven to be reliable, such that a transfer can be sent half way round the world and be received within a day.

For small value purchases, however, banker's drafts are still used. These are foreign denominated cheques drawn on the banks' accounts. They are mostly used by students to pay for college fees and purchase of books. However, with the advent of electronic debit cards, there is bound to be less use of the facility, especially where speed is of the essence. With debit cards, transfers are instant, whilst drafts have to be sent by post and could take time to reach the beneficiary. The risk of the instrument being lost in transit cannot be ruled out as well.

One cannot fail to notice the growth in use of mobile banking. Banks have made very good use of advances made in mobile phone technology and have incorporated it into their systems. With mobile phone having sophisticated software of a computer, it has been transformed from being a mere tool to carry out a verbal conversation. Access to personal bank accounts has been made possible, and one is able to carry out various financial transactions. Some of the available services are fund transfers, balance enquiries and mini statements. Requests can be made for statements and cheque books as well.

This is a very secure service, as long as one makes sure that the assigned Personal Identification Number (PIN) is not given to any other person. Unfortunately, the usual practice has been sharing PINs for debit cards and mobile phones with close relatives, which has led to dire consequences when funds on accounts are accessed fraudulently.

Internet banking has also been made available, though limited access to internet facilities has limited its use. This could however change shortly, since internet facilities are available on mobile phones.

The other instrument used in funds transfer, especially in international trade, is the letter of credit. This is a document issued through a bank, and in the case of Zambia, combined with a standard guarantee form duly filled in and signed by the bank. The guarantee is an assurance that a seller would receive payment in full on condition that all the stipulated delivery terms are met. The letter of credit is cash covered, meaning that an equivalent amount of cash is kept aside by the bank in case of the buyer failing to pay.

A letter of credit is appropriate to use in international transactions, as buyers and sellers often do not know each other, and are probably not aware of how laws are in each other's country regarding international trade. They may also not be aware of each other's creditworthiness. The bank therefore steps in to minimize these risks.

There are international rules regarding the letter of credit, which the bank acting on behalf of the buyer will make sure are followed, and all the conditions met before payment is made to the seller.

Letters of credit handled by banks in Zambia are irrevocable, meaning that they cannot be amended or cancelled without mutual consent of all parties.

For the bank to effect payment, the seller must provide documentary proof that goods have been dispatched and are of the correct quantity and of the required quality. Typical documentation presented might include;

1-a bill of exchange

2-invoices or packing lists

3-shipping documents

4-origin and inspection certificates

5-bill of lading or airway bill or forwarder cargo receipt

6-insurance certificate

The fact that actual documents have to be presented in order to take control of the goods has limited the use of electronic transmission in letters of credit transactions. Imaging of documents is mainly used for record keeping.

Since international trade involves high values, most banks have dedicated departments and staff dealing with these transactions, just to ensure that no financial loss is suffered by the bank or customer due to clerical error.

3-SOFTWARE PACKAGING

There has been as much pressure on software developers as there has been on banks to be innovative in order to meet customers' demands. It has been recognized that each customer has a unique need, maybe totally different from the rest. This has led to banks to tailor products according to the needs of customers, not just delivering standardized ones across the segments.

In order to stay in business with the banks, software developers have had to tailor their products along the same way, developing software packages that do not only meet the needs but also leave room for expansion. Other factors that have to be considered are that banks operating across different territories may have subsidiaries or branches working on totally different software platforms. Developers therefore have to consider how their packaged product is going to interface with these platforms without causing disruptions to bank business.

The operating landscape for banks and software developers

is not the same as it was five years ago. As fresh needs arise, customers continue to look for products that will meet their needs at an affordable price. Operating software for banks has developed to levels that were not thought possible just a few years ago.

Since the start of the reformation of the payment system in Zambia, major advances have been made. Developers have looked at various functions within the bank and packaged their software accordingly. This has resulted in banks having one platform that is able to accommodate all the workload and functions of all the departments.

The current situation is that front and back office functions have now been integrated in the system so as to enable a person switch between the two at will and in no time. The branch computer system may consist of a teller terminal in, say, Kitwe, connected to the branch server, which in turn is connected to a central server in Lusaka. It could alternatively be a situation where a teller in Lusaka is connected directly to the central server in the same city. In both cases, access to the central server will always be available, though the link with the branch server in Kitwe could be slow at times.

What the banking system is really aiming for is direct transmission of electronic transaction files without a break in the system, a seamless kind of processing called Straight-Through-Processing (STP). There is no human intervention in this kind of electronic processing, thus reducing on fraud and human error.

There is a drive towards a continuous online system, connecting with the clearing house at all times. The current network set up may not allow this at the moment, but this may be achieved through the use of optical fibre technology, connecting the banks' central server with the clearing house.

The front office system in most banks has a range of functions. A teller can deal with enquiries, work on cash withdrawals and deposits, as well as deal in foreign transactions. Real Time Gross Settlement (RTGS) and SWIFT payments can also be made, as well as ordering cheque books and scanning of signatures and mandates.

Cashiers are usually restricted to dealing with cash deposits and withdrawals, as well as cheque deposits. RTGS and SWIFT payments, ordering of cheque books and scanning of documents are usually assigned to other counters, such as Enquiries.

In the branch banking halls, customer service staff will have access to account opening functions that also incorporate in requirements relating to Know Your Customer (KYC), Anti-Money Laundering (AML) and compliance functions.

The banking system expects a software package that includes treasury department functions, for the purpose of fund management, as well as corporate department for its interaction with customers who are connected to the bank servers for their daily monitoring of accounts and fund transfers. The package should be secure and reliable, and should be able to interface with other different software packages that customers may be using in their offices.

4-OVERVIEW-process change

It cannot be emphasized that in today's environment, the banking industry is faced with greater challenges than ever before. There is an onslaught of regulatory requirements in an increasingly risk aware environment. Both market and customer requirements are changing rapidly. Bank management has no option but to closely scrutinize not only on returns on investments but also have time to market and successfully address business requirements. With so much now being invested in technology, all eyes are focused on teams in charge of computer systems and there has been a lot of pressure on them to deliver successfully, within budget and on schedule.

Facing these types of challenge has forced banks to be flexible and agile in both strategy and operations. It must be noted that throughout history, redefining processes have changed the business landscape (Vijay Alexander, 2008).

Process is now a key concern for business managers and

technology architects, and not just for work study experts or auditors. It is now a critical requirement in the financial services industry, which has opted for a process centric approach using pre-built processes with leading practices, components and services. Arguably, it is much easier to define and implement processes in manufacturing, rather than service industries, though this view is now being challenged. In manufacturing, a product's inputs and the output remain fairly uniform, regardless of where it is produced. In service industries such as banking, the service is much more variable, depending on where it is offered and by whom (Eapen Thomas, 2008)

The term 'process centralization' has a variety of meanings in several fields. In political science, centralization refers to the concentration of a government's power both geographically and politically into a centralized government. In neuroscience, centralization refers to the evolutionary trend of the nervous system to be partitioned into a central nervous system and peripheral nervous system. In business studies, centralization and de-centralization refer to where decisions are made in the chain of command. In this case, the concentration of management and decision-making power is at the top of an organization's hierarchy.

Furthermore, the location of all or most main departments and managers are at one facility. For our purpose, centralization is the process by which the activities of an organization, particularly those regarding planning and decision making become concentrated within a particular location and/or group. It is the act or process of combining or reducing several parts into a whole (Vijar and Eupen 2008). Centralization involves bringing together key activities in one particular part of an organization. This might be, for example, at Head Office.

Centralization may further convey the idea of consolidation, amalgamating, integration, concentration, aggregating, integration and combining of processes. Centralization has also been viewed as mapping multiple processes and data of an organization and generating a comprehensive integrative structure. (Klaus et al., 2000).

Generally, the banking sector is experiencing unprecedented demand and fierce growth. Local banks therefore need to respond instantly to their customers' needs and offer highly targeted and innovative products if they are to maintain or build their market position. Unfortunately, and especially as regards local banks, their infrastructure is generally the legacy of several decades of ad hoc investment in locally-sourced solutions that may not be up to the rigors of the international banking world. As a result, they experience a lot of difficulties in their quest to offer competitive and targeted products quickly and to grow business using existing platforms.

For financial services institutions to react quickly to business and market changes, there has to be a significant reduction in their cost base, possibly by rationalizing their IT infrastructures in addition to centralization of processes. In doing so, they will improve their competitiveness. Locally-built legacy core banking systems have been identified as a key factor limiting future growth and adaptability. As stated before, forward-thinking banks are now strategizing to using components of packaged core banking solutions to re-engineer their existing solutions to manage higher volumes, compete in an intensely competitive market place, and reduce margins and to meet increased customer expectations effectively (Financial Insights 2008)

5-CASE STUDIES

Driving factors or causes of process centralization in the banking industry are brought out in the following case studies:

Case Study 1

Allianz Bulgaria operates in a fiercely competitive market and in a predictable macroeconomic environment with sustainable growth. The bank's existing core system had been sourced from a local vendor and had reached the end of its functional life. It was based on as outdated MS DOS platform which had its own database structure. This made it difficult for the system to interface with other vendors' software. In addition, it operated on an entirely decentralized system, working through approximately 40 different banks before consolidating information at head office. A key requirement was to centralize the back office, IT and support functions to free up personnel in the bank's outlets for customer service and sales.

In 2006, the bank took a strategic decision a common platform. The aim was to become the best bank in the assurance business. The key driving factors behind this decision were as follows;

1-the bank needed a system that could support a new banking business model and strong annual growth. Allianz bank was aiming for an annual growth rate of 30% in Bulgaria. The existing platform could not bring competitive new products to market fast enough. It was also difficult to offer customers individually tailored products such as flexible deposits and loans. To ensure business growth, Allianz bank needed an easily scaleable system.

2-In order to maintain its competitive edge, the bank realized that it had to offer targeted and innovative products to its customers. A key factor in achieving this goal was to find a way to easily develop new products and bring them on the market.

3-the bank was unable to offer services tailored to its customers, such as flexible deposits and loans.

4-Keeping abreast of its business and ensuring compliance with a growing range of national and international regulations required a system that would enable bank staff to quickly access information relating to all parts of the organization and generate reports. The bank believed that a system based on Oracle technology would help it achieve these goals.

5-Allianz Bulgaria needed a system that would enable it to target its products at individual customers. Technology that would be able to interface with Customer Relationship Manager and other satellite systems was therefore essential.

6-the bank needed to complied with the IT policy of the Allianz group. The solution therefore had to be designed by a company with international expertise. However, it also required a local support system that could understand the nuances of the local Bulgarian banking market. All these requirements presented a very compelling set of business drivers for change.

As stated earlier on, the bank's business ambitions were to have a centralized IT functionality. This could only be realized if the new system was the right solution with the right functionality and support. Allianz Bulgaria therefore set out to select its facilitator of change, seeking one that would demonstrate global experience as well as at least one successful installation in local market. This needed to be backed up by a local implementation team which could provide a system of high quality, but at a competitive price (Financial rights 2008).

Case Study 2

A leading global bank sought to consolidate its global network services vendor base by centralizing global procurement of goods and services, deployment, support and operations services with a limited number of strategic global IT services partners. It also sought to mitigate potential regulatory risks brought about by regional inconsistencies in technology services and support. The bank also believed that the optimum way to achieve real efficiencies, service improvements and cost reductions would be to combine supply (including deployment), support and operations under one global vendor with a proven track record and experience in these areas.

Working collaboratively with Dimension Data, the bank took the decision to establish a global programme to ensure effective co-ordination and timely delivery of the transition, and to ensure a focus on continual improvement, delivered to the best levels of service at both a local and global level. Dimension Data referred to this approach as its GOLD standard, Global Orchestration Local Delivery; which delivers the leverage that globalization provides, while ensuring that local relationships remains intact (Dimension Data 2011).

Case Study 3

Shared service centres were initially formed to help

companies centralize and re-engineer core processes to improve cost efficiency and financial and risk management. Payments are often the first such core processes to be centralized into Shared Service Centres. These have had an impact on treasury operations. The landscape of processes for centralization has now widened to what were previously regarded as core treasury functions. Although these are frequently geographically distinct from central treasury, in low-cost locations in central and Eastern Europe, the technology underpinning Shared Service Centres has allowed specific parts of end-to-end processes to take place despite being located in different geographical areas.

Cost reduction and efficiency improvements remain a central goal of the Shared Service Centres, but other objectives have also become important as their operational capability improves and additional functions are included, such as foreign exchange and liquidity management. Since 2008 increasing risk management capability has also been a critical goal of Shared Service Centres. The emergence of the Shared Service Centre has meant that operating models have needed to be redesigned. This has been shaped by drivers specific to business models and industries, including technology capability, geographical footprint and, most importantly, customers.

If, for example, the Shared Service Centres adds another business entity in execution of a process, it will require new management mechanisms, such as service level agreements

(SLAs) and key performance indicators (KPIs) to ensure alignment and operational effectiveness. While the uncertain economic environment is a key driver in expanding the use of Shared Service Centres for more effective information management, technology is no longer the only key factor.

Increased regulation and changing market structures are also driving significant change. The introduction of the single euro payments area (SEPA) with its 1st February 2014 end date prompted companies to add centralized receivables to Shared Service Centres. They also ensured that the applicable cut-off time for processes through the Single Euro Payment Area was observed. In short, SEPA required compliance. It became mandatory as of 1st February 2014. Companies had to ensure that they met the requirements so that they could make payments and collections, and their business continue to function.

Case Study 4

In 2006, Schroder Private Banking undertook a project to centralize its IT and support infrastructure into one central hub using the Tremenos' T24 core banking system. Established in London in 1804, Schroder is one of the world's oldest and most venerable financial institutions. It has run as a private family business for over 150 years. With active involvement of the founding Schroder family, the company's stable ownership has translated into consistent returns and sustained growth. As at the end of December 2008, Schroder operated from 34 offices in 26 countries, employing more than 2,800 people and managing assets worth more than GBP110 billion.

Schroder Private Banking is part of the Schroder group, and operates chiefly out of three locations, London, Zurich and the Channel Islands, although it has offices in other European cities and a growing presence in Singapore. According to public filings, Schroder Private Banking has experienced strong growth in margins and profitability in recent years. Between 2006 and 2007, the bank's cost/income ratio improved by 15% and its operating margin increased by 38%. This led to the bank achieving a 54% rise in operating profit over the same period. As at 31 December 2008, Schroder Private Banking was managing GBP11.7 billion of clients' funds and employing more than 300 people.

Given this background, the question arises as to why Schroder's Private banking should choose to centralize its IT systems.

The decision to centralize the group's IT infrastructure was taken as a result of a study carried out to determine how an increase in operational efficiency could be achieved. There was an additional question of what needed to be done to maximize synergies within the group. The findings highlighted the following:
-The business models varied considerably between the different banks – the London bank, for example, had a

higher share of discretionary services than either the Swiss or Channel Islands banks with more advisory and custody driven activities.

-The different models had resulted in substantially different IT infrastructures and cost bases.

-There was significant room to reduce the complexity of the IT infrastructure and improve business processes by centralizing and harmonizing systems. The existing Swiss platform was characterized by a high level of automation, thanks in a large part to having adapted its processes to the functionality in T24 without significant local developments.

It was found that a Shared Service Centre was the best way to achieve this centralization. This would result in better profitability, improved customer service, faster product innovation and superior risk management and compliance. A decision was made to merge IT infrastructure and operations of the three banks into a shared service centre in Zurich, with T24 acting as the core processing application (and supported by only a few ancillary applications). Zurich was chosen because it already managed the operations for private banking in both Zurich and Geneva and part of the institutional business based in Zurich, at a competitive cost level.

It was planned that all accounting, security and payments services for clients, including custody operations, maintenance of client data and IT (infrastructure, development and maintenance), would be handled from

Zurich, while all front office services and client activities as well as compliance and legal services and treasury were to remain under the control of the local entities.

Schroder Private Banking embarked on this transformational IT project at the end of 2005. The T24 was used as the core banking software. As stated above, the key driving factors for undertaking this project were multi fold: a reduction in operational costs, enhancement of customer service, increase product innovation and improve risk management and compliance. Management projection was that by using the Shared Service Centre in Zurich, total operating costs could be cut by one third, as against the cost of maintaining the three standalone IT and support centres (Tremenos, 2011)

Case Study 5

The State Bank of India (SBI), the largest and oldest bank in India, had computerized its branches in the 1990s, but it was losing market share to private-sector banks that had implemented more modern centralized core processing systems. To remain competitive, the bank began implementation of a centralized core system in 2002.

Tata Consultancy Services was selected to customize the software and implement the new core system. Implementation of the Tata Consultancy Services BaNCS Core Banking at the State Bank of India and its affiliate banks represented the largest centralized core system implementation ever undertaken. A total of 140 million accounts held at 14,600 domestic branches of SBI and its affiliate banks had to be converted.

The State Bank of India is the oldest and largest bank in India, with more than United States $250 billion in assets. It is the second-largest bank in the world in number of branches. It opened its 10,000th branch in 2008. The bank has 84 international branches located in 32 countries and approximately 8,500 ATMs. Additionally, it controlling or complete interest in a number of affiliate banks, resulting in the availability of banking services at more than 14,600 branches and nearly 10,000 Automatic Teller Machines.

The bank traces its heritage to the 1806 formation of the Bank of Calcutta. The bank was renamed the Bank of Bengal in 1809 and operated as one of the three premier "presidency" banks (the presidency banks had the exclusive rights to manage and circulate currency and were provided capital to establish branch networks). In 1921, the government consolidated the three presidency banks into the Imperial Bank of India.

The need for centralization of the system arose because of deficiencies noted in its existing platform. In 1990, massive computerization had been made, to automate all of the branches. A highly customized version of Kindle Banking Systems' Bank master core banking system was implemented. However, because of the bank's historic use of local processing and the lack of reliable telecommunications in some areas, it deployed a distributed system with operations located at each branch. Although the computerization improved the efficiency and accuracy of the branches, the local implementation restricted customers' use to their local branches and inhibited the introduction of new banking products and centralization of operations functions.

Furthermore, the local implementation prevented the bank from easily gaining a single view of corporate accounts, and management lacked readily available information needed for decision making and strategic planning. The advantages in products and efficiency of the private sector banks became increasing evident in the late 1990s as the bank, as well as other public sector banks, lost existing customers and could not attract the rapidly growing middle market in India. In fact, this technology-savvy market segment viewed the public sector banks as technology laggards who could not meet their banking needs.

As a result, the Indian government sought to have the public sector banks modernize their core banking systems. In response to the competitive threats and entreaties from the government, the State Bank of India engaged KPMG Peat Marwick (KPMG) in 2000 to develop a technology strategy and a modernization road map for the bank. In 2002, bank management approved the KPMG-recommended strategy for a new IT environment that included the implementation of a new centralized core banking system. This effort would encompass the largest 3,300 branches of the bank that were located in city and suburban areas. The State Bank of India's objectives for its project to modernize core systems included:

1-delivery of new product capabilities to all customers, including those in rural areas
2-unification of processes across the bank to realize operational efficiencies and improve customer service
3-provision of a single customer view of all accounts
4-ability to merge the affiliate banks into State Bank of India
5-provision of support for all State Bank of India existing products
6-a reduction in customer wait times in branches
7-stopping the trend of losing customers.

John M. Floyd is the chief executive officer of John M. Floyd & Associates. This is a Houston-based bank profitability consulting firm with 30 years' experience and serving more than 1,400 financial institutions. John began his consulting career after serving as a profit planning manager of Texas Commerce Bank. His observations were that the key element toward insuring proper credit discipline in banks is development of a strong centralized credit administration department. Once that department is in place, it will be amazing to note how much more time the rest of the staff will devote to enhancing the sales culture. This move can go straight to your bottom line. For a bank, this means having a strong centralized credit administrator function that can help ensure proper credit discipline. If this department fulfills its responsibilities, it will effectively remove the "back room" work from the loan platform and support the bank's lenders and provide them with additional time to focus on bank's sales culture (John M Floyd 2003).

Case Study 6

Oracle announced that BankABC has gone live with Oracle FLEXCUBE Universal Banking Solution as a state of the art banking platform on which to support its retail and corporate banking operations. BancABC, previously known as African Banking Corporation, operates branches in five countries; Zimbabwe, Zambia, Botswana, Tanzania and Mozambique.

Offering a diverse range of financial services including personal, business and corporate banking as well as asset management, stock broking and treasury services, the bank needed to upgrade its banking platform in order to take advantage of additional features and the latest technology within Oracle FLEXCUBE universal banking while also reducing maintenance costs and enabling it to take new products and services to the market in a timely manner. The Oracle FLEXCUBE Solution has allowed BancABC to consolidate its banking environment and remove separate solutions focused solely on its retail banking branch by bringing all operations under one common platform. The highly scaleable infrastructure provided by the Oracle FLEXCUBE solution has enabled BankABC to consolidate its retail and corporate banking operations into one robust banking platform with standardized business processes and centralized banking operations.

Oracle FLEXCUBE universal banking solution first went live in January 2011 and has now been rolled out across all the five countries of operation, the last one having gone live in November 2011. Oracle FLEXCUBE was seen as an obvious choice for their bank since they were looking to bring retail and corporate operations onto one platform. This was the best way to serve their customers who are across multiple markets. The bank needed to invest in a scaleable and flexible core banking platform to reflect the current market conditions, as well as prepare for the future.

In summary therefore, the main driving factors for process centralization in the banking industry can be said to be increased regulation, mitigation of potential regulatory risks and achievement of real efficiencies. The others are service improvements and cost reductions.

Other factors include operational efficiency, improved customer service, better profitability, faster product innovation, improve risk management and compliance, response to competitive threats and government entities. The need to take on new products on the market on the timely manner also plays a large part, as well as the reduction of maintenance costs. In this ever changing environment, businesses also see the need to change business models which may be outdated and need rebuilding or redesigning.

6-BENEFITS arising from process centralization.

Bulgaria

Deployment of the system was done efficiently and on time. Logical integration was also effectively done, with the systems for internet banking, cards, SWIFT and Bulgarian payments interfacing easily with the new platform. The bank now enjoys a secure, centralized and easy-to-use IT system that responds to change quickly, enabling it to launch new products quickly.

The bank has already benefited from some of the advantages of the system with an increasing number of electronic channels and higher client and employee satisfaction. Furthermore, cost reduction was achieved through reduction of staff numbers from 54 to 28, affecting 126 branches. This left staff to concentrate on front line sales. Improvements were also noted in bank closing times. There were no late working hours, resulting in a boost of staff morale. Costs relating to late working hours of staff were also reduced.

(Financial rights 2008)

Leading Global Bank

Regional inconsistencies in technology services and support have been largely eliminated. This has ensured that all regional-specific regulatory requirements are currently being addressed. Dimension Data has been able to identify and continuously address reporting and tracking challenges. Through proactive monitoring and reporting, they have been able to filter the type of alerts and threshold breaches to continuously improve the network's performance. Standardized work packages for repeatable ad-hoc project service requests further improve levels of consistency. The burden of overseeing day to day operations has been lifted from the bank's internal team.

Transparency of operations has been delivered through regular reporting. Access to relevant and real time information is also now possible through online systems. Restructuring and streamlining of procurement, delivery and support of its global networks services has ensured that the bank consistently meets its cost reduction targets.

By conducting regular assessments, Dimension Data has been able to meet the bank's expectations for continuous refinement, improvement and technology optimization. A recent quote from the client provides testimony to the depth and quality of the partnership in place, "Dimension Data is helping to manage not only the risk, and costs in technology organization but is also key in helping change the organizational structure and culture globally".

The bank is assessing how to further leverage and scale the global delivery and support platforms, with Dimension Data as its primary partner.

Collection of financial instruments has always been difficult to rationalize because of the use of different payment instruments and reconciliation methods in different countries. An example of collection of an instrument would be when Bank A, located in Zambia, receiving a cheque deposit from its customer, the cheque being drawn on Bank B, located in another country with no local branch in Zambia. Bank A would have to send the cheque on a collection basis, to Bank B through the post or express mail, with instructions to credit its account once the funds are cleared by Bank B.

Single Euro Payment Area does away with many of those requirements. Payments and financial instruments sent on collection basis are the same throughout the 27 EU countries, the three European Economic Area (EEA) member countries and both Switzerland and Monaco. Moreover, there is standardization of clearing procedures. However, companies are also using the opportunity presented by Single Euro Payment Area to audit where they make collections and which parts of the business are involved.

The Single Euro Payment Area can therefore be used as a catalyst to drive change across the business, as well as an opportunity to improve collections efficiency. Single Euro Payment Area also offers the promise of improved reconciliation and account rationalization, which has long been a priority for many treasury departments. This can be achieved through having clearer guidelines on how information is presented in specific fields. Similarly, for those companies with appropriate organizational structures, Single Euro Payment Area enhances the benefits of payments and receivables on behalf of structures because it removes the need for many local bank accounts (Lesley white and Bruce Meull, 2013).

Benefits in the case of Schroder Bank

1-the IT architecture was greatly simplified, with a number of software applications cut by 63%.
2-access of management information improved considerably.
3-there was a marked improvement in customer service. Customer statements are now sent out a week earlier than before.
4-there is better management of risk, and the bank has been able to adhere to compliance directives.
5-operating costs have reduced significantly.

The move to centralization has allowed Schroder to run the bank's operations much more tightly. Much of this operational improvement is clearly reflected in the lower cost base per transaction. However, moving to the centralization has also enabled bank management to obtain better quality information that, in turn, allows it to make better informed decisions about the business. The challenges regarding allocation of resources between competing priorities have also been eased. As Heinz Scheiwiller pointed out, information has improved in three key ways:

1-by using consolidated data from all three banks and applying the same level of analysis to all three entities, Schroder has been able to compare financial data more easily and more accurately, not just across the different banks, but also at the individual customer level.

2-the bank has moved away from arbitrary cost allocation between the different banks and profit centres because data available is more granular and consolidated. Instead, costs are now allocated in a way that reinforces the accuracy of profit measurement.

3-the centralization has enabled the quality of information to improve and be timely. Higher levels of automation coupled with the absence of reconciliation between different data sources means that Schroder can now perform the monthly consolidation for the entire bank within a few days when the need arises.

In general terms, the move to centralization has improved customer service in a number of ways. It has permitted customer relationship managers to spend more time with customers. This is because IT related time burdens are done away with. It has also allowed the bank to increase the proportion of relationship managers to customers.

Relationship managers now have access to real time desktop client information. Furthermore, customers are now able to get more detailed and timely performance information reports. In terms of more specific Key Performance Indicators, though these vary according to the kind of service, Schroder has achieved marked improvements in most. For example, the most important Key Performance Indicator is the cost of transaction. Since going live, Schroder has substantially reduced this.

There was a sense of product innovation as customers of all of the banks have benefited as the move has resulted in Schroder taking the best products and practices from the three constituent banks and rolling them into one standard, but more extensive offering. The standardization of the range of products has also ensured greater efficiencies at the operational level.

Client reporting is another area that has improved significantly since operations were centralized, and an area where Schroder has been able to differentiate itself from its competitors. As stated before, Schroder is able to send out client statements about a week earlier than before. Furthermore, while all statements have a similar format, a fact that allows the bank to leverage its branding more strongly than before, the flexibility of the integrated system allows the content of the client reports to be tailored to individual client specifications.

Probably the best aspect of centralization has been the elimination of the big discrepancy that used to exist in the operating costs of the different platforms. Schroder is now running an extremely lean infrastructure, with costs lower by approximately one third, and with IT support in the service centre representing only about 5% of the total workforce. Efficiency gains were mainly driven by a reduction in staff numbers. Of the total cost reduction, approximately 60% came from reduced staff numbers. The remaining 40% of cost savings stemmed from non-staff related costs, principally lower software maintenance costs and reduced hardware spending.

IT now accounts for less than 10% of total costs and 5% of the total workforce. At the moment, there is now only one back office, one securities master, one client static data administration team and one dealing desk, as opposed to three or more in each case before the IT centralization project.

The cost of monitoring activities like compliance has also decreased. Only having one processing location means that Schroder is in a position to deliver any requested information in these areas in a short timeframe as many of the underlying data delivery processes have been simplified. Additionally, having one consolidated back office centre reduces operational risks, as well as the risks of non-compliance, in that there is more management oversight.

More importantly, though, is that management now has access to better, more aggregated information with fewer errors. This information is being received quicker than before. Better informed decisions can therefore now be made about the business, helping to mitigate risks (Heinz Scheiwiller).

The State Bank of India

The new core system has resulted in benefits throughout the bank for both the customers and the employees of Sate Bank of India. For example, the new core banking system has allowed the bank to redesign processes. It established 400 regional processing centers for all metro and urban branches that have assumed functions previously performed in the individual branches. The bank recently reported that business per employee increased by 250 percent over the last five years.

The bank has also achieved its goal of offering its full range of products and services to its rural branches. It delivers economic growth to the rural areas and offers financial inclusion for all of India's citizens. In fact, the bank recently completed the consolidation of State Bank of Saurashtra into State Bank of India. The trend of losing customer has now been reversed, and the bank is now gaining new market share.

Completion of the core conversion project has also allowed the bank to undertake several new initiatives to further improve service and support future growth. These initiatives include the deployment of more than 3,000 rural sales staff and redesigning of over 2,200 branches in the last fiscal year. Additionally, more than 1,000 new branches have been opened and a call centre established.

BankABC

The advanced architecture of the Oracle FLEXCUBE solution enables it to easily interface with third part systems, including the bank's retail branch applications, meaning that a clear picture of all its operations across multiple countries can be obtained easily.

Oracle Financial Services Software was able to meet the challenges that came their way. By offering a standardized and centralized system such as FLEXCUBE, it enabled BancABC to integrate all its operations and provide a better service for its customer.

From the above highlighted reviewed case studies, it's clear that the benefits included customer satisfaction, risk management, reduction of operation costs, and standardization of processes, improved management information and addressing regulatory requirements.

7-CHALLENGES arising from centralization.

In the case of Bulgaria, it was noted that data needed to be 'cleaning', because the previous system did not have any control over account creation. As a result, customers were often entered into the system multiple times from different locations. Time therefore had to be dedicated to cleaning all duplicate customer and account entries. The bank also discovered a lot of inactive accounts. Owners of these accounts had to be notified about the closure of the accounts. It took an estimated six to seven months to complete this exercise.

The bank also had to upgrade its communications bandwidth and network, moving to Multiprotocol Label Switching (MPLS) layer 3 connectivity. Although this was done on time, there was the challenge of finding a company that could provide this level of coverage throughout the country. It discovered that the national Telco was the only one.

A lot of patience needed to be exercised with the performance of the database at first, as it was initially very slow when it went live. The bank also realized that more time was needed to train staff for them to feel confident with the new system and become familiar with the change. At the outset, it was thought that two months would be sufficient for the training, but after the implementation, it became obvious that this wouldn't be enough.

The change to a new system also meant changing people's habits. Challenges were experienced during stress testing. Although these were done before going live, not all staff participated. The bank therefore had to be more proactive before going live to avoid unnecessary costs. What had to be emphasized on was that training was intense and testing needed to be done accordingly.

The other challenge had everything to do with change management and cultural differences. While some members of staff responded positively to the change, others in the branches were resistant to the programme (Financial Rights 2008).

In the case of Schroder Bank, the challenges faced related to staff being made redundant. There was the specific challenge of how the bank would ensure the affected staff's continued cooperation with the project, and how to ensure a smooth and complete knowledge transfer. Data migration to the new system in particular, proved to be very challenging. Lack of integration in the past had resulted in accumulation of a lot of redundant and inconsistent data, and there was often no unique relationship across the applications (Heinz Scheiwiller 2009).

For State Bank of India, challenges included finding a new core system that could process approximately 75 million accounts daily, a number greater than any bank in the world was processing on a centralized basis. Moreover, the bank lacked experience in implementing centralized systems. Its large employee base took great pride in executing complex transactions on local in-branch systems. This practice led some people to doubt that the employees would effectively use the new system.

Another challenge was meeting State Bank India's unique product requirements. That meant making extensive modifications to a new core banking system. The products included gold deposits, savings accounts with overdraft privileges, and an extraordinary number of passbook savings accounts (The Tower Group, 2009).

Some writers have admitted that centralization of processes is not a simple task. There are hurdles that have to be bound over, both within and outside the organization. While some specific issues are unique to each organization, common ones typically include:

1-resistance to centralizing,

2-lack of focused expertise

3-multiple and conflicting strategies

4-undefined procurement roles

Some of the key challenges that banks face when trying to deliver to both business and regulators include:

1-complexity in the form of functional overlaps

2-multiple systems with similar data that cannot provide a single customer view

3-end-to-end process integration, where a customer can be uniquely identified across the organization

4-chaotic point-to-point interfaces, requiring significantly longer change projects and higher costs.

This makes the road to consolidation a rocky one. Furthermore to exacerbate the situation, most organizations do not have a consistent and documented architecture, therefore, "current state" is not well understood. There are no consistent methodologies and standards applied across the whole bank and no IT governance processes, or even if there are, such processes are loosely applied with the discretion of each division (Bruno and Apeshi, 2004).

With some organizations, policing and application of policy could be weak. Information and data from internal and external sources is usually allowed to grow exponentially over a period of time. The vast amount of data collected is held in tens, if not hundreds, of different systems, formats and data models with masses of duplication. There is simply no consistent enterprise wide data architecture.

In a nutshell from the highlighted cases, and what other researchers have written, the following seem to be the challenges of process centralization:

-change is involving and time consuming,
-new systems could be slow at the beginning,
-more time is needed to train staff,
-staff members need to familiarize with change,

The organizations need to put in place change management to combat issues like cultural differences and staff redundancies. To ensure continuity, there should be smooth and complete knowledge transfer. Effective data migration requires that those in charge are experienced in implementing centralized systems.

There will also be customer uncertainty which bank management will have to deal with, as well as product requirement, undefined procurement roles and multiple and conflicting strategies. Lack of focused expertise could derail the centralization project.

Centralization is not a simple task. Large-scale core systems implementations are typically the most costly and risky IT projects undertaken by banks. Failures of core systems projects are not uncommon at large banks. This results in loss of both financial business opportunities. Furthermore, failed projects causes banks to delay needed core systems replacements, because they measure the risk of failure against the potential benefits of a new system (Tower Group, 2009)

8-EFFECTS of process centralization

The pressures on the employees of banks around the world have been manifold across financial systems. Factors that bring these about are numerous, such as entry of new players and products with advanced technology, globalization of financial markets, changing demographics of customer behaviour, consumer pressure for wider choice and cheaper service, shareholder wealth demands, as well as shrinking margins. Centralization of processes, among other strategies, is most widely used by firms to strengthen and maintain their position in the market place.

It is considered to be a relatively fast and efficient way to expand into new markets and incorporate new technologies, though we can still find that success of the process is by no means assured. A majority of these changes fall short of their stated aims and objectives. Some failure can be explained and justified by financial and market factors, but a considerable number can be traced to human resources issues and activities.

There are numerous studies, which confirm the need for firms to systematically address a variety of human resource issues, activities and challenges. It is a natural phenomenon that a dissatisfied employee cannot bring efficiency (Dr K. A Goyal; Vijay Joshi, 2012).

Based on data for twenty O and ECD countries, research has shown that performance can either increases or decreases with centralization, depending on the ability of the higher levels of an organization to bind the lower ones.

Employee commitment is a concept which has attracted much attention in recent years. Research has focused on relationships between commitment and various facets of individual performance and on the psychological basis of the commitment itself. It profiles the pattern of employee commitment found in an exploratory study of employees of a large retail bank which is undergoing a process of both structural and cultural change. Three bases of employee commitment were found to be; internalized commitment; identification commitment and compliance commitment. These are profiled against the pattern of commitment which the literature suggests will be found across various employee grades.

Evidence from the exploratory research has been presented which suggests that major change may result in the dissolution of internalized commitment on the part of employees, coupled with a corresponding increase in compliance commitment (Dr Tanai Khiaonarong; Dr Jonathan Liebenau, 2009). The closure of bank branches to reduce operating costs has resulted in the restructuring of the established industrial labour relations to create greater workplace flexibility and competitiveness in the banking industry. There are no more 'jobs for life' and full-time employees may be replaced with part-time or temporary workers (Leyshon & Thrift, 1993; Pollard, 1995; Wills, 1996).

There has so far been little systematic tracking of job losses resulting from domestic mergers and centralization. Focus is almost exclusively on financial, competitive, consumer/customer and shareholder considerations. A domestic merger and process centralization provides the ideal occasion to review cost and revenue structures as a basis for planning and implementing new processing and staffing arrangements. The obvious need to harmonize the human resource practices of two organizations and to rationalize overlapping functions also provides persuasive arguments for job cuts to eliminate duplication.

Job losses in individual firms are usually exacerbated by increased use of information and communications technologies in the newly centralized organization and the outsourcing of functions previously performed by employees. The pressure to reduce costs, especially fixed costs and to adopt flexible staffing and work methods has had a pervasive effect on employment. Continuing efforts to reshape the boundaries of firms through mergers, centralization and outsourcing have further contributed to job insecurity.

Financial institutions around the world are not only closing traditional outlets as a result of mergers and centralization but are also reducing staff at remaining offices by making use of new technology to overhaul back office and other support operations.

There has been a decline in permanent employment, increased job instability and insecurity, and rapid growth of various non-standard forms of work, including part-time and temporary employment. Critics also claim that the current spate of mergers are resulting not only in massive lay-offs but also in financial exclusion for an increasing number of communities whose branches are closed and reduced personal service without any corresponding reductions in service fees and other charges.

Observers also note that, while merger-related lay-offs can generate cost savings, this may be at the risk of disrupting operations, leaving staff adrift and the organization unable to respond to new threats or opportunities. During the course of integration, companies may realize their projections were over-ambitious and that the implementation of the full retrenchment programme could seriously jeopardize the ability of the enterprise to respond to changes in the economic environment. Furthermore regulatory constraints and industrial relations considerations may induce organizations to adjust their initial plans (Paul Montent, 2001)

9-CRITICAL SUCCESS FACTORS

In the case of Schroders Bank, various initiatives were used to address the issue of motivation, and to assist the knowledge transfer (especially regarding the locally different legal, tax and client reporting requirements), Schroders used a mix of computer based training programmes, leaflets, intranet information and classroom teaching. There was excellent cooperation throughout the project between the London and Channel Islands based staff and the staff in the service centre in Zurich.

Finally, there is the question of time commitment. A Shared Service Centre typically requires a two to three year commitment for the project to be fully implemented, depending on the size and complexity of the organization, as well as a significant investment in companywide systems. Companies could significantly reduce this time frame in a bank consolidation exercise, which is why they should not overlook this option. Other critical success factors noted from State Bank of India are:

1-senior management commitment. The project was driven by the chairman of State Bank India, who met every month with the information technology (IT) and the business sector heads. The chairman monitored the overall status and ensured that sufficient resources were allocated to the project. TCS senior managers were thoroughly committed to the project as well and periodically met with the State Bank of India chairman to review the project status.

2-staffing and empowerment of project team. The core banking team consisted of the bank's IT managing director acting as the team leader, with 75 business people and IT staff members selected by the bank. TCS also staffed the project with approximately 300 IT professionals trained on the Banks' system. Most importantly, the State Bank of India business people were viewed not just as contributors to a key project but as future bank leaders. This team reported to the State Bank of India chairman and was empowered with all decision-making authority.

3-ownership by business heads. The regional business line heads were responsible for the success of conversion of their respective branches and reported the status to the chairman. The business heads' objectives were thus aligned with those of the project team.

4-focus on training. SBI used its network of 58 training centres across India to train employees on the new system.

TCS personnel first educated approximately 100 SBI professional trainers, who then trained the remaining 100,000 SBI employees at the centres (Tower Group, 2009).

Other researchers have pointed out that for a successful centralization to be carried out, all hurdles must be overcome by strong leadership, disciplined strategy and ability to successfully prepare for the challenges ahead. With a strong leader guiding the effort to centralize and an understanding of expectations, the rewards at the end will prove to be worth the effort.

10-THEORETICAL FRAMEWORK

The consolidation of bank processes around the globe has fuelled an active public policy debate on the impact of consolidation on financial stability. Economic theory provides conflicting predictions about the relationship between the market structure of the banking industry and the fragility of the banking system.

Some theoretical arguments and country comparisons suggest that a less concentrated banking sector with many small banks is more prone to financial crises than a concentrated banking sector with a few large banks (Allen and Gale, 2000, 2003).

The pure centralized model implies that there exist more than one level of organization, and that decisions are made only by at the highest level. No decisions are made at lower levels. On the other hand the pure decentralized model is a single level model which operates without any central authority and implies the existence of more than one centre of decision making. The problem of both centralization and decentralization of decision making has for a long time played a fundamental role on the theory of the functioning of the socialist economy (Janusz G Zielinski, 1963).

The decentralized model usually includes a strong global treasury centre as the hub, or treasury headquarters. This site provides general ground rules to all decentralized operations by way of global policies and guidelines. While the decentralized model solves many of the problems that expansive global treasuries face, this model has its own challenges.

A decentralized treasury structure typically requires more aggregate global treasury personnel than a centralized structure, and the model still presents some challenges to the headquarters' treasury level in areas of communication and oversight. In these difficult economic times, the added costs of redundant staffing, maintenance of multiple treasury sites and systems can be a challenging economic hurdle to overcome. Because of these issues, many treasurers have moved to a centralized treasury structure.

Both the centralized and decentralized treasury structures offer advantages and disadvantages. Which design a company chooses will depend on global footprint, available resources, executive commitment, and available technology. Regardless of which centralization path treasurers select, a successful implementation will hinge on their ability to secure prior senior management buy-in, a well-defined plan, and sufficient resources to implement the project. Once in place, and to remain successful, each structure will require:

1-strong and clear global policies, effective tools and technology
2-effective ongoing management reporting, with well-trained and capable personnel.

With an effective treasury structure and capable resources, treasury can support even the most challenging demands that a global business can present (John Herrick & Michael Gallans, 2010). A theory of decentralization and centralization noted that under centralization, localities are vertically integrated with a benevolent central authority who effectively possesses all property rights while under decentralization, localities are separate legal entities (endowed with property rights) who bargain to determine the project size. We can examine the performance of these two regimes and attempt to show how one or the other may dominate depending on the distributions of private and external benefits from the project.

The effect of the size and variation in the externality on this trade-off is of particular interest. The Coase theorem states that in the absence of transaction costs, the central authority only has to assign and/or enforce property rights of the concerned agents, and bargaining between the agents will generate an efficient outcome. Both these approaches lead to efficiency when there are no market imperfections of any sort. If there are imperfections, however, the comparison between these two modes of regulation becomes more complicated. If, for example, the central authority is imperfectly informed about the social costs and benefits of the project, it has to extract this information from the informed agents before putting in place its regulatory scheme. Similarly, if agents are asymmetrically informed, this will affect the outcome of bargaining between them.

Since the two approaches may behave quite differently in the presence of asymmetric information, the problem of choosing the better one is not trivial. The main difference between these two approaches is in the attribution or not of property rights, to the regulated agents. Under a centralized scheme, property rights are retained by the centre which imposes a solution on the agents. Under a decentralized scheme, agents are endowed with property rights which they can trade or bargain with.

An example of a centralized rights structure is the portrait of a centralized regime as depicted by De Long and Shleifer (1993) who study the impact of centralization of power on economic growth in European cities between 1050 and 1800. They define a centralized absolutist regime as one where "subjects have no rights, they have privileges, which endure only as long as the prince wishes." In such a setting, there are no enforceable agreements or bargains. The central authority can always break the promise (Peter Klibanoff;

Michael Poitevin, 2013) The term "decentralization" embraces a variety of concepts which must be carefully analyzed in any particular country before determining if projects or programs should support reorganization of financial, administrative, or service delivery systems.

Different types of decentralization should be distinguished because they have different characteristics, policy implications, and conditions for success. Types of decentralization include political, administrative, fiscal, and market decentralization. Drawing distinctions between these various concepts is useful for highlighting the many dimensions to successful decentralization and the need for coordination among them. Nevertheless, there is clearly overlap in defining any of these terms and the precise definitions are not as important as the need for a comprehensive approach.

Political, administrative, fiscal and market decentralization can also appear in different forms and combinations across countries, within countries and even within sectors. According to the 2013 study guide, centralization is said to be a process where the concentration of decision making is in a few hands. All the important decision and actions at the lower level, all subjects and actions at the lower level are subject to the approval of top management. According to Allen, centralization is the systematic and consistent reservation of authority at central points in the organization. The implication of centralization can be reservation of decision making power at the top level, reservation of operating authority with the middle level managers and reservation of operation at lower level at the directions of the top level. Under centralization, the important and key decisions are taken by the top management and the other levels are into implementations as per the directions of top level.

Taking a business concern as an example, the father and son being the owners decide about the important matters, but the rest of functions like product marketing, finance marketing and personnel, are carried out by the department heads, and they have to act as instructed ordered by the top two people. Decision making therefore remains in the hands of father and son. On the other hand, decentralization is a systematic delegation of authority at all levels of management, and in all of the organization. In a decentralization concern, authority is retained by the top management for taking major decisions and framing policies concerning the whole concern. The rest of the authority may be delegated to middle and lower levels of management.

The degree of centralization and decentralization will depend upon the amount of authority delegated to the lowest level. According to Allen (2003), decentralization refers to the systematic effort to delegate to the lowest level of authority, except that which can be controlled and exercised at central points. Decentralization is not the same as delegation. In fact, decentralization is an extension of delegation. Decentralization pattern is wider in scope and the authorities are diffused to the lowest most level of management.

Delegation of authority is a complete process and takes place from one person to another, while decentralization is complete only when the fullest possible delegation has taken place. The general manager of a company is, for example, responsible for receiving the leave application for the whole of the concern. The general manager delegates this work to the personnel manager who is now responsible for receiving the leave applicants. In this situation delegation of authority has taken place. On the other hand, if the general manager delegates this power to all departmental heads at all levels upon the request of the personnel manager, then decentralization has taken place.

There is a saying that "Everything that increasing the role of subordinates is decentralization and anything that decreases the role is centralization". Decentralization is wider in scope and the subordinate's responsibility increase in this case. On the other hand, in delegation the managers remain answerable even for the acts of subordinates to their superiors. (Allen C Carison, 2010).

According to Fayol's principle, centralisation means that authority is concentrated at the top level of management. In other words, centralization is a situation in which top management retains most of the decision making authority. Decentralization means that decision making is distributed among all levels of the organization. This means that information is shared from the top of management downwards.

According to Fayol, the degree of centralization or decentralization depends on a number of factors like the size of the business, the nature of the business, the experience of supervisors, the dependability of workers, and the ability of the workers. Fayol believed that total centralization and decentralization is impossible, and that organizations should strive to strike a balance between the two. In conclusion, Fayol was a strategist. He wanted to make the work place a better place for everyone. He believed that there should be one central point in the organization which exercised overall direction and control of all parts, but the degree of centralization of authority should vary depending on the situation. Fayol's principles were intended to be a guide for managers to use while also pursuing efficiency, order, and stability.

Fayol's ideas were revolutionary during his time. His ideas and principles influenced the way management thinks.

Centralization can improve working methods in that all staff has access to standardized support services so that they receive equal treatment regardless of where they work. On the other hand, where decentralization works effectively, it can help alleviate the bottlenecks in decision making that are often caused by central government planning and control of important economic and social activities.

Decentralization can help cut complex bureaucratic procedures and it can increase government officials' sensitivity to local conditions and needs. Moreover, decentralization can help national government ministries reach larger numbers of local areas with services, allow greater political representation for diverse political, ethnic, religious, and cultural groups in decision-making, and also relieve top managers in central ministries of routine tasks to concentrate on policy. In some countries, decentralization may create a geographical focus at the local level for coordinating national, state, provincial, district, and local programs more effectively and can provide better opportunities for participation by local residents in decision making.

Decentralization may lead to more creative, innovative and responsive programs by allowing local experimentation. It can also increase political stability and national unity by allowing citizens to better control public programs at the local level. It is, however, not a panacea, and it does have potential disadvantages. Decentralization may not always be efficient, especially for standardized, routine, network-based services. It can result in the loss of economies of scale and control over scarce financial resources by the central government.

Weak administrative or technical capacity at local levels may result in services being delivered less efficiently and effectively in some areas of the country. Administrative responsibilities may be transferred to local levels without adequate financial resources and make equitable distribution or provision of services more difficult. Decentralization can sometimes make coordination of national policies more complex and may allow functions to be captured by local elites. There may also be distrust between public and private sectors, which could undermine cooperation at the local level.

Project and program planners must be able to assess the strengths and weaknesses of public and private sector organizations in performing different types of functions. Before developing elaborate plans for decentralization, they must assess the lowest organizational level of government at which functions can be carried out efficiently and effectively and for functions that do not have to be provided by government, the most appropriate forms of privatization.

Even program planners who do not see decentralization as their primary motive must carefully analyze the types of decentralization already present in a country in order to tailor policy plans to existing structures. In most countries an appropriate balance of centralization and decentralization is essential to the effective and efficient functioning of government. Not all functions can or should be financed and managed in a decentralized fashion. Timeless as the tug of war between centralization and decentralization is, it remains a dilemma for most companies to help senior managers make better choices about what to centralize and not to centralize (Andrew Campbell, Steplen kuncsch, 2011).

The idea of the centrality of individuals and organizations in their social networks was one of the earliest to be pursued by social network analysts. The immediate origins of this idea are to be found in the sociometric concept of the 'star', that person who is the most popular in his or her group or who stands at the centre of attention. The formal properties of centrality were initially investigated by Bavelas (1950), and, since his pioneering work, a number of competing concepts of centrality have been proposed. As a result of this proliferation of formal measures of centrality, there is considerable confusion in the area. What unites the majority of the approaches to centrality is a concern for the relative centrality of the various points in the graph the question of so-called 'point centrality. From this common concern, however, they diverge sharply. A number of measures of point centrality need to be reviewed, focusing on the important distinction between local and global point centrality.

A point is locally central if it has a large number of connections with the other points in its immediate environment if, for example, it has a large neighborhood of direct contacts. A point is globally central, on the other hand, when it has a position of strategic significance in the overall structure of the network. Local centrality is concerned with the relative prominence of a focal point in its neighborhood, while global centrality concerns prominence within the whole network.

Related to the measurement of point centrality is the idea of the overall 'centralization' of a graph, and these two ideas have sometimes been confused by the use of the same term to describe them both. Freeman's important and influential study (1979), for example, talks of both point centrality and graph centrality. Confusion is most likely to be avoided if the term centrality is restricted to the idea of point centrality, while the term 'centralization' is used to refer to particular properties of the graph structure as a whole. Centralization, therefore, refers not to the relative prominence of points, but to the overall cohesion or integration of the graph.

The first big conceptual trouble in understanding Chandler's argument at the structural level is that centralization and decentralization as Chandler uses them are really two different kinds of centralization. For one thing, centralization is for administering one product with losses and profits over the central authority, and for another, centralization is for administering one product for one market with both market and administrative controls.

In recent years, decentralization has received widespread attention as a major element in the discourse on 'good governance', promoted by many donor agencies and development institutions (Bergh 2004). Decentralization has many functions. From the point of view of 'good governance', it is a mode of administration that advocates bottom-up planning which captures, internalizes and addresses local needs and concerns (Johnson 2001; Devas 2002). As such, it promotes responsiveness and accountability of policy makers to local needs and people (Crook & Manor 1998). They must create or maintain the enabling conditions that allow local units of administration or non-government organizations to take on more responsibilities.

Central ministries often have crucial roles in promoting and sustaining decentralization by developing appropriate and effective national policies and regulations for decentralization and strengthening local institutional capacity to assume responsibility for new functions. The success of decentralization frequently depends heavily on training for both national and local officials in decentralized administration.

Technical assistance is often required for local governments, private enterprises and local non-governmental groups in the planning, financing, and management of decentralized functions. Much of the decentralization which has taken place in the past decade has been motivated by political concerns. In Latin America, for example, decentralization has been an essential part of the democratization process as discredited autocratic central regimes are replaced by elected governments operating under new constitutions.

In some countries, such as Ethiopia, decentralization has

been a response to pressures from regional or ethnic groups for more control or participation in the political process. In the extreme, decentralization represents a desperate attempt to keep the country together in the face of these pressures by granting more autonomy to all localities or by forging asymmetrical federations. A variation of this theme has been the view of decentralization being an outcome of long civil wars, such as in Mozambique and Uganda, where opening political opportunities at the local levels has allowed for greater participation by all former warring factions in the governance of the country.

The transition economies of the former socialist states have also massively decentralized as the old central apparatus crumbled. In many countries, decentralization simply has happened in the absence of any meaningful alternative governance structure to provide local government services. In some cases, particularly in East Asia, decentralization appears to be motivated by the need to improve service delivery to large populations and the recognition of the limitations of central administration.

Although the main reason for decentralization around the world is that it is simply happening, there are a multitude of design issues that affect the impact of different types of decentralization on efficiency, equity and macro stability. In this regard, there is a growing body of literature examining the economic rationale for decentralization. The specific services to be decentralized and the type of decentralization will depend on economies of scale affecting technical efficiency and the degree of spillover effects beyond jurisdictional boundaries. In practice, all services do not need to be decentralized in the same way or to the same degree. In an important economic sense, the market is the ultimate form of decentralization in that the consumer can acquire a tailored product from a choice of suppliers.

The nature of most local public services limits this option and establishes a government role in ensuring the provision of these services, but it does not automatically require the public sector be responsible for the delivery of all services. Where it is possible to structure competition either in the delivery of a service, or for the right to deliver the service, evidence indicates that the service will be delivered more efficiently. In comparison, it has not been as easy to centralize the daily operational tasks of maintaining bank accounts, monitoring cash inflows and outflows and investing short-term funds.

There are external legal, tax and banking issues, and internal political/personnel issues that constrain centralization. Many established companies with existing financial operations in multiple countries find vested local interests that resist centralization efforts. As a result of this, most companies have established regional centres, not global centres, to coordinate and perform international cash management activities. This has become most common in the Eurozone where the introduction of the Euro since 1999 has led to the opportunity for concentration of euro-denominated funds. The concept of pan-regional cash management activities has extended especially to the Asia Pacific region. There are, however, hurdles in these very heterogeneous regions that are more pronounced.

11-CONCEPTUAL FRAMEWORK

Consolidation of business entities or indeed consolidation of processes is a worldwide phenomenon. It is most motivated by technology innovation, deregulation of financing services, enhancing intermediation and increase emphasis on shareholders' value, privatization and international competition (Berger et al, 1991; De Nicole et al...2003;).

The process of consolidation has been argued to enhance bank efficiency through cost reduction revenue in the long run. The pattern of banking system consolidation could be viewed in two different perspectives, namely, market driven and government led consolidation.

The market driven consolidation which is more pronounced in the developed countries sees consolidation as a way of broadening competitiveness. This is with added corporate advantage in the global context and eliminating excess capacity more efficiently than bankruptcy or other means of exit. On the other hand, government led consolidation stems from the need to resolve problems of financial distress in order to avoid systematic crisis as well as to restrict inefficient banks (Ajayi, 2005:2).

To keep the head high in globalized economy, one has to follow the path of growth, which contains various challenges and issues. One has to overpower these challenges and issues to become a success story. However such structural changes in financial system can have some public policy implications (Dr K.A Goyal; Vijay Joshi 2012).

12-RESEARCH FINDINGS

Causes for centralization

Findings from a research carried out regarding the reasons for centralizing processes are as follows:

1. Efficiency/timeliness

 28% of the respondents observed that the reason why their bank/institution centralized their processes is to enhance efficiency.

2. Cost effectiveness/optimal allocation of resources

20% of the respondents emphasized that the cost effectiveness or optimal resource allocation is a valid reason for financial institutions to centralize their processes.

3. Risk mitigation

32% of the respondents emphasized that the risk mitigation that would accrue to the banking institution is a valid enough reason why its processes should be centralized.

4. BOZ regulatory policy

8% of the respondents emphasized that the compliance with the Bank of Zambia regulatory policies is the reason why commercial banking processes and systems should be centralized.

5. Non Applicable Response

12% of the respondents never indicated their opinions on the reasons for centralization of processes.

The above analysis is supplemented with qualitative analysis as submitted by the respondents during the research as follows:

-Having one central processing place so as to fit in their competitive market

-staff and operational cost reduction

-improvements in controls and accountability

-improvements in operational efficiency levels

-risk mitigation. In order to minimize business risk and errors, changes are made to improve controls and effect monitoring to improve turn-around time on processes

-segregation of duties and improvement on transparency in processes involved

-to avoid duplication of cheque image processing and improve efficiency and standardization of cheque clearing period.

-to reform and enhance the payment system for example cheque truncation had to be complied with.

It was observed that of the total number of respondents to the questionnaire given out, only 4% indicated that they were positively impacted by the process centralization implemented by their employer bank. On the other hand 96% was impacted negatively when their banks centralized its operational processes.

78% of the respondents indicated staff insecurity as the major effect on employees following centralization, 6% indicated low staff morale, another 6% of the respondents indicated high labour turnover and 10% of the respondents indicated a *laisser faire* attitude as the effect of process centralization on employees

-No proper time taken to implement centralization process. Centralization is mostly done without taking into account mitigation measures.

-Most experienced staff is laid off because some units have been done away with. In the process, the organization loses excellent skill and knowledge.

-Customer facing staff (in customer service roles) is unable to meet customers' expectations because of delays in processing time from a central point.

-Personal circumstances making staff deployment difficulty, and staff morale is negatively impacted in some cases because of uncertainty.

During the research, it was also observed that other negative effects of centralization on employees are as follows:

1. Time Delay

31.6% of the respondents indicated that the effect of a centralized banking institution's processes has been that longer time is taken to process transactions.

2. Process incompatibility

10.5% of the respondents indicated that the effect of a centralized banking institution's processes is incompatibility between the branches and the central processing point.

3. Staff insecurity

26.3% of the respondents indicated that the effect of a centralized banking institution's processes is a work force with a growing propensity to seek greener pastures, hence resulting in a very high staff turnover rate. This has a negative impact on the employees.

4. Indifference

31.6% of the respondents indicated indifference on the effect of centralizing of banking processes.

-Delay in work processing: Processing time had increased due to referring transactions to a central point. Even routine tasks like payment of monthly bills tend to be slower, which has in turn created a negative relationship with the institution's suppliers.

-There have been delays in meeting deadlines and turn around tine before a process is completed. There is also time wastage at point of decision making. Since staff members at central point are not customer facing, they tend to move at a slow pace in service delivery.

-Central processing units are overwhelmed and in the process fail to meet service level agreements with other departments. Central processing staff may also not fully understand the systems, and ownership of the processes becomes a challenge.

-Staff displacements may be caused by certain roles falling off. This in turn causes movement of staff from one area to another at a cost which may turn out to be expensive.

-People resisting the change may delay the process adoption.

-There may be quantity disagreements between the central point and ultimate users

Delay in work processing caused by referring transactions to one central point. It has made bill payment slower which has in turn created a negative relationship with the institution's suppliers.

-There have been delays in terms of meeting deadline and turnaround time before a process is completed. Since staff at central point is not customer facing, they tend to move at a slow pace in service delivery.

-Central processing units being overwhelmed, and in the process fail to meet service level agreements with other departments. Processes from a decentralized perspective, hence delaying flow of most central processing staff understanding the systems and work, and not owning their work.

-Lack of due diligence and phased approach

-Staff displacements; certain roles falling off causing movement of staff from one area to another at a cost; so it's expensive.

-People resisting the change hence delaying the process Adaption and employee frustration.

-Quantity disagreements between central point and ultimate users

Centralization among other strategies is most widely used by firms to strengthen and maintain their position in the market place. It is considered to be a relatively fast and efficient way to expand into new markets and incorporate new technologies.

The benefits of centralization of processes observed from the research are as follows:

1. efficiency/timeliness

40% of the respondents emphasized that benefits in terms of efficiency would accrue to the banking institution if its systems centralized.

2. Cost effectiveness/optimal allocation of resources

20% of the respondents emphasized that benefits in terms of cost effectiveness or optimal resource allocation would accrue to the banking institution if its processes were centralized.

3. Risk mitigation

18% of the respondents emphasized that benefits in terms of risk mitigation would accrue to the banking institution if its systems were centralized.

4. System Standardization

12% of the respondents indicated that benefits in terms of system standardization would accrue to the banking institution if its systems were centralized.

5. Customer service

8% of the respondents indicated that benefits in terms of customer service delivery would accrue to the banking institution if its systems were centralized.

The above analysis is supplemented with qualitative analysis as submitted by the respondents during the research as follows:

Process centralization would bring about the following advantages:

1. Uniformity in processing of various transactions.

2. Ease of monitoring workflow

3. Improvements in operational efficiency because of timely execution of instructions and ownership of responsibility

4. Cost reduction

5. There are checks and balances that ensure that funds are not mismanaged

6. Payments being done on time, for instance cheque clearing period being reduced

7. There is reduced staff movement from branch to the clearing house. Staff can concentrate on other value adding initiatives

8. There is quality work, and job roles are well defined. Specialized staff whose expertise is valued is employed. There is also re-allocation of responsibility from a busy branch to a central point for action.

9. Discounts being obtained on bulk buying;

-A lot of due diligence should be carried out in a phased way, and other options available are examined

-Before implementation of centralization, parallel systems should be run to identify flaws in the new system. More often than not, when a process change occurs, there are numerous system errors that crop up, either denying customers access to their accounts or funds. If the change involves migration of accounts to another system, there could be duplications of accounts or omissions. Either way, customers are inconvenienced. If the process involves funds transfer systems, monies usually end up in suspense accounts that take ages to reconcile. In addition to denying customers access to these funds, there is the risk of fraudulent withdrawals from these accounts by unscrupulous staff members whilst the change process is in progress.

-It would be more effective if a bank maintained centralized processing while allowing peripheral offices to have sufficient authority on a certain level of processing. A limit could be put in place, for instance, on procurements and bill payments such that transactions within, say, K10,000.00 are processed in the branch/centre. Any amount above that should be done through the central finance or accounting department to ensure checks and balances.

-The line of authority should be structured in such a way that decision making can be made without delays. Authority should not be left in the hands of a few individuals.

-Centralization of processes should be in-country, as opposed to totally outside the country.

-It should be ensured that all stakeholders are involved in the centralization process, involving all units to get ideas from them and not just imposing process centralization on them.

-Systems should be up-to-date, tested and staff trained to understand the implications of the centralization process.

-Centralization must only be implemented after a successful pilot project.

ABOUT THE AUTHORS

Mercy Mwila Kunda holds a Bachelor of Science degree in Banking and Finance obtained from the Copperbelt University. She is a banker of more than fifteen years experience.

Julius B Goode also holds a degree in Banking and Finance, and has more than twenty years experience in banking.